HAYNES EXPLAINS
THE FRENCH

Owners' Workshop Manual

 • Written by **Boris Starling**

Published in September 2017

A catalogue record for this book is available from the British Library

ISBN 978 1 78521 154 6

Haynes Publishing, Sparkford, Yeovil,
Somerset BA22 7JJ, UK
Tel: +44 (0) 1963 440635
Website: www.haynes.com

Haynes North America, Inc.,
861 Lawrence Drive, Newbury Park,
California 91320, USA

Printed and bound in Malaysia

Cover image from Getty Images

Illustrations taken from the
Haynes Citroën 2-cylinder
Owners Workshop Manual

Written by **Boris Starling**
Edited by **Louise McIntyre**
Designed by **Richard Parsons**

Safety first!

It is imperative to adhere to certain stringent safety measures with the French.

a) When eating, do not ask what part of an animal the food comes from. You almost certainly don't want to know.
b) When drinking, affirm constantly that you have never tasted such exquisite wine anywhere on your travels.
c) When driving, either outsource it to a local or watch *Mad Max* beforehand.
d) When making love, remember to remove your socks beforehand.

Working facilities

Working facilities? You're joking, aren't you? This is the French we're talking about. Yes, technically they work 35 hours a week, but take away 14 for lunch, another 10 for flirting, six more for shrugging and then five for general recalcitrance, stroppiness and arguments leaves zero. So it doesn't really matter what the facilities are like. Work is very much an abstract concept round these parts. Going on strike, on the other hand, is something at which they're absolutely world-class.

Contents

Introduction

In the beginning, God created France. (He had meant to create Spain first, but he figured there was no rush and he could do it mañana.) And when he looked at France, he was pleased with what he'd done. It was the most beautiful country in the world: it had mountains and beaches, forests and plains. Its weather was perfect for making the finest wines imaginable, and he could already envisage the site where the City of Light would be built.

Yes, he thought: France was just about perfect.

Except for one thing. All this beauty in one place – it wasn't fair that one country should have it all. He had to even things up somehow.

So he created the French.

About this manual

The aim of this manual is to help you get the best value from the French. It can do this in several ways. It can help you (a) decide what work must be done (b) tackle this work yourself, though you may choose to have much of it performed by external contractors such as the armed forces of the United States and United Kingdom, who had to come in at short notice – twice – to clear up the mess left by the cowboys from Muller, Schmidt & Schneider who left the place in a dreadful state. But that's all spilt milk under the bridge, or another mixed metaphor of your choice, and we're all friends again now, aren't we?

The manual has drawings and descriptions to show the function and layout of the various components. Tasks are described in a logical order so that even a novice can do the work, which should prove useful to those who never bothered to learn French at school and think that the best way to make themselves understood abroad is either by **SHOUTING VERY LOUDLY** or speaking

Very

Slowly

Indeed.

 Dimensions, weights and capacities

Overall height

Eiffel Tower	324m
Napoleon	Just looked short as his bodyguards. were so tall, alright?
Baguette	65–100cm. Non, I will not convert that into your perfidious English imperial measurements.

Overall weight

Parisian women	50kg (by law)
Frenchman minus ego	75kg
Frenchman plus ego	175kg

Consumption

Brie and other types of cheese	24 tons per person per year.
Burgundy, Bordeaux etc.	They know where the EU wine lake is and they're not telling you.
Filterless Gauloises	20 per day, rising to 30 once you become a teenager.

Engine

Stroke	Bien sur. Normally between 5pm and 7pm with someone who is not your spouse.
Power	Germany has it all. Sometimes they let the French have a little for a day or so.
Torque	About philosophy. While wearing black polonecks. In chic cafés.
Bore	Gaston in the corner over there. Always going on about how that was never a penalty for Paris St. Germain and how the ref should have gone to LunetteSauveurs.
Redline	When reached, silent but haughty and disdainful.

Model characteristics

The average Frenchman (who will of course tell you there is no such thing, as all Frenchmen are exceptional in every way) believes he's the greatest lover since Casanova (an honorary Frenchman), the greatest chef since Escoffier, the greatest warrior since Napoleon and the greatest singer since Chevalier. In many cases there is not the slightest evidence for any of these claims.

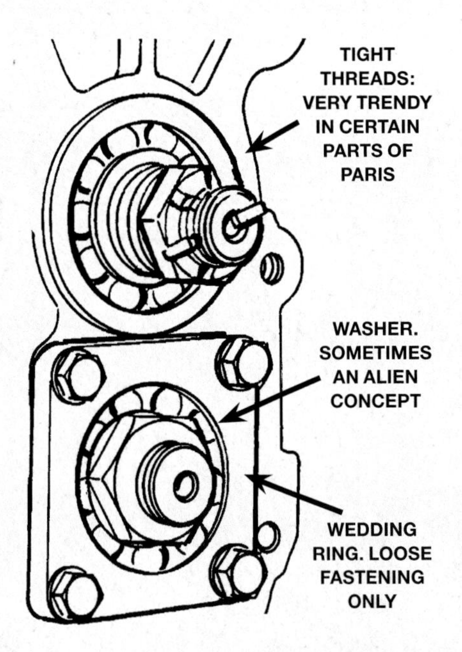

FIG 7•1 **SOONER OR LATER IT ALWAYS COMES BACK TO SCREWS**

The Frenchman

Frenchmen especially aspire to be 'intellectuels', in whom the French retain a touching faith and who always give their opinions on the matters of the day – even (or especially) when they have no direct knowledge of said matters. The last time the British tried this kind of thing was with the C4 programme *After Dark*, which was intended to be a high-minded discussion of current affairs but was instead hijacked by a hammered Oliver Reed who propositioned one fellow guest and challenged another to a fight.

The link between intellectuals and politics in France works both ways. With tensions running high between France and the US over Iraq in the early Noughties, the then French Foreign Minister Dominique de Villepin published an 800-page book.

About poetry.

Revenge

In the olden days, one Frenchman who wanted to take revenge on another had two choices: write a biting epigram or challenge him to a duel. Basically, if you were hacked off with Jacques, you either had to shoot him or write 'Jacques smells of poo-poo' on a wall.

 The Frenchwoman

The Frenchwoman is a superior species to her male counterpart, not least because she constantly makes him believe that she isn't.

1) She looks good, no matter where she is or what she's doing. The very notion that one might do the school run in tracksuit bottoms and without make-up would have the Frenchwoman re-enacting Munch's 'The Scream.'

2) She's well-organised. She doesn't get flustered: why else are both panache and sangfroid French words? She compartmentalises: she works when she's at work but wouldn't dream of replying to emails from home late at night or reading a book while on an exercise bike in the gym.

3) She eats three meals a day but stays thin, because she eats at regular times, doesn't snack and stops eating when she's had enough.

4) She tells it like it is. She doesn't intend to be offensive, just truthful. If she thinks you look a state, she'll tell you. While looking absolutely stunning herself, of course.

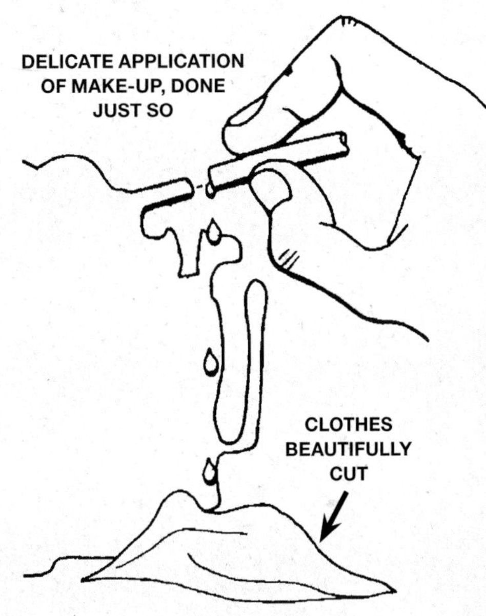

FIG 7•2 **THE FRENCHWOMAN'S DAILY ROUTINE**

5) She raises polite children who greet adult visitors with a kiss on each cheek and then sit listening in silence. (Most English people have never seen this happen outside a Julie Andrews movie.) French children therefore learn early that grown-ups are extremely boring. This is a lesson that they will pass onto their own children at the earliest opportunity by making them sit through tedious property-prices-and-politics chat.

The horn

Any discussion of Frenchmen and Frenchwomen leads naturally onto sex, which is, come to think of it, where most things in France lead sooner or later.

The French think of sex as fun, natural, and nobody's business but that of the consenting adults involved. Sex for the French is a fundamental human urge, like hunger or thirst. For a people so keen on wearing elegant and well-cut clothes, the French are equally keen to disrobe at the drop of a hat.

The French regard adultery as an occupational hazard of being married. A little dalliance, nothing serious or permanent? Bien sûr, not just for your sake but more importantly for your partner's too. The French have affairs not to destroy marriages but to save them. Cheating is one thing; hurting someone you love or causing them to lose face is quite another. When the Monica Lewinsky scandal broke, the French struggled to see what Bill Clinton had done wrong. He lied? Of course he lied. That's what a gentleman does.

Cynics might note that the national symbol of France is the cockerel, famous for seducing many hens and crowing triumphantly afterwards irrespective of whether he's satisfied them or not. The Frenchman's answer to this, as indeed to most things in life, is perhaps the single most French thing of all – more French than Roquefort, Burgundy and Serge Gainsbourg put together.

It is, of course, the Gallic shrug.

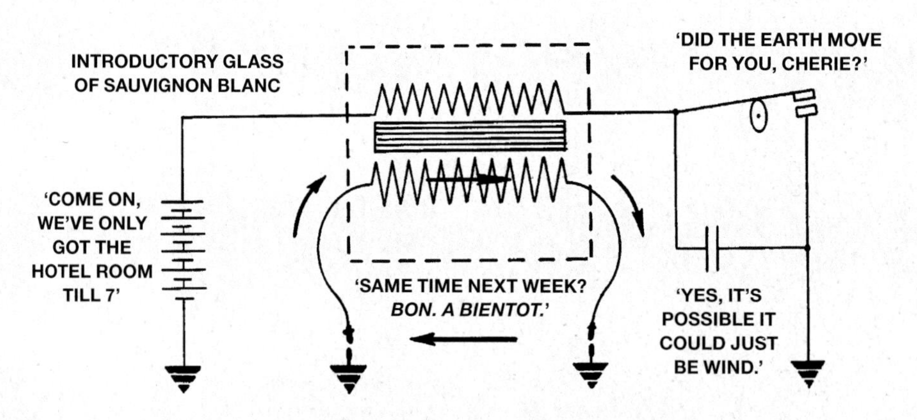

FIG 7•3 **THE *CINQ-A-SEPT* SEISMOGRAPH**

⚠ The Gallic Shrug

The Shrug is like tightrope walking or concert piano playing. It looks easy, but that's only because the people doing it are experts who've put in many thousands of hours' practice. Don't assume that you can just do any old shrug with a stupid face and expect to pass as a local. Don't be a have-a-go-hero.

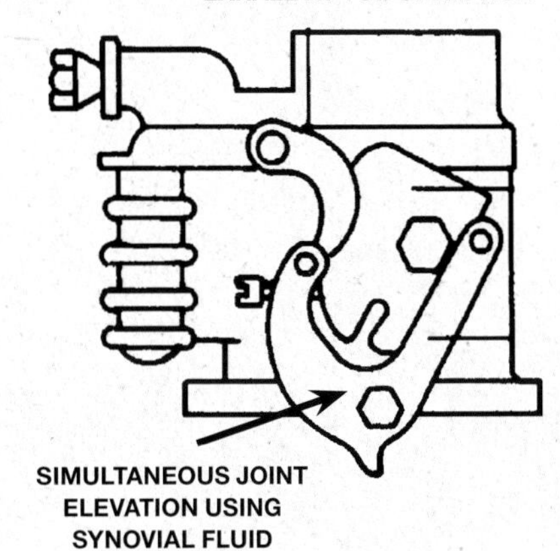

FIG 7•4 **BILATERAL SCAPULAR MOVEMENT MECHANISM**

1) Think French. The shrug is as much state of mind as gesture.
2) It takes only a second to go from repose to Full Shrug, but a lot has to happen in that second. Get even one of these stages wrong and the knock-on effect can be catastrophic.
3) Start to hunch your shoulders.
4) Bring your palms up and over so they're facing upwards.
5) Tilt head slightly to one side (choice of side optional).
6) Raise eyebrows. If in doubt, watch Roger Moore in any Bond film.
7) Purse lips and exhale. The sound should be a soft raspberry 'bof.'
8) Maintain for a split second and relax.

You'll need to practice in front of a mirror before trying this out in public. Even then, your first attempts will be awkward and unconvincing. But one day someone'll ask you a question, you'll instinctively bof-shrug and your French friends will look at you with new respect and a little awe.

Not that they'll show it, of course. They'll just shrug.

WARNING

Do not attempt the Gallic Shrug when located outside French territory. People will think you're either deranged or have an incurable bodily tick.

Road manners

Calm. Safe. Considered. Slow. Selfless. Literally none of these adjectives apply to French driving.

There's a famous short film called *C'était un rendez-vous* in which a car roars through Paris at insane speeds, narrowly missing pedestrians, driving the wrong way up one-way streets, running red lights, mounting the pavement and so on. Most of the world regard it as a bravura and daring piece of performance art. The French see it as a basic training manual for learner drivers.

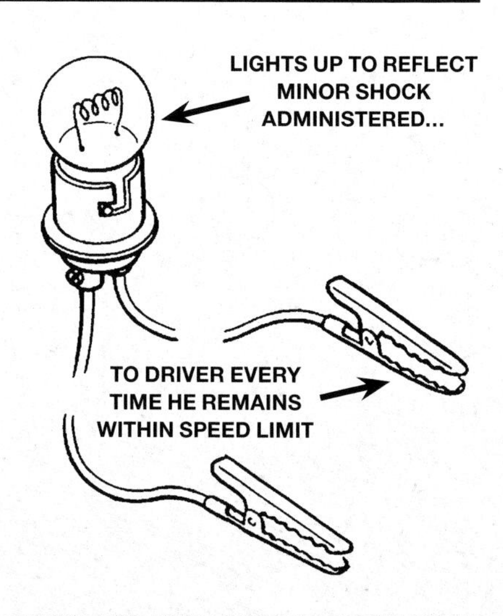

FIG 7•5 **SPEED LIMIT CIRCUIT CONTROLLER**

When driving in France...

a) Speed limits are either strictly advisory or refer to the minimum speed at which you can travel.

b) When cornering, follow the racing line. This will probably take you onto the other side of the road. In most countries this would be a problem, but since in France everyone coming the other way will also be following their racing line onto your side of the road, you'll be fine.

c) There's no French word for 'indicator'.

d) Priority is technically to the right, but as any fule kno, might is right. Give way to anything bigger than you. End of.

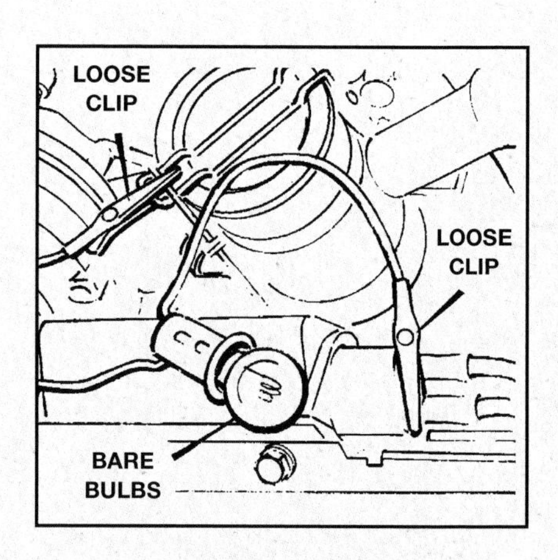

FIG 7•6 **STANDARD QUALITY CONTROL FRENCH WORKMANSHIP.**

e) When taking a right turn off a roundabout, it's much better to go the wrong way round ¼ of the roundabout than the right way round ¾ of it.

f) Use your brakes sparingly and your horn abundantly.

g) If you can still see the numberplate of the car in front, you're too far away. Five millimetres away at 95mph is the sweet spot.

h) The perfect parking place causes maximum inconvenience to most people. Half on the pavement and half on the road, with not quite enough room for pedestrians on the inside and other cars on the outside, is the gold standard.

i) Give all foreign-registered cars a wide berth except for the Italians, who alone in Europe know how to drive like the French.

j) Can't quite fit into a parking space? No problem. Reverse into the car behind and nudge it gently backwards until you have enough space. Of course, you should be prepared to find this happen to your car in turn while you're away from it. If you come back to your parking space and can't find your car, don't worry. It probably has been neither nicked nor impounded; it's just four or five car spaces away from where you left it. Look, it's just there, between Gaston's ancient Renault and Mme. Pompadour's 2CV.

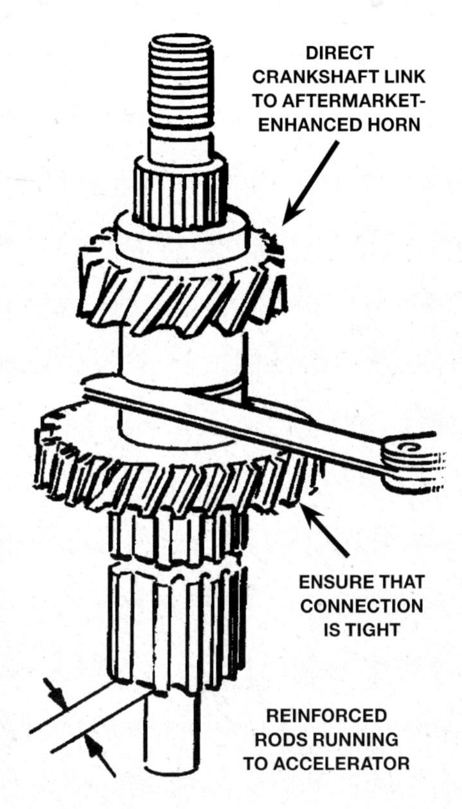

FIG 7•7 **MAKING YOUR CAR ROADWORTHY IN FRANCE**

Pedestrian crossings are designed to keep the population fit by ensuring they can break into a sprint at will.

Interior

The French see themselves as very blessed to be French (though not blessé, which is French for 'wounded', which is in turn what they will be if you suggest that being French is not the greatest thing in the world).

No matter how much a Frenchman may like you, a foreigner, he will still at heart pity you for not being French. They are the most civilised, most intelligent, most cultured and most beautiful people ever. They believe they have given the world much of what is regarded as civilisation these days; not just their culture but also their political ideas of liberty, equality and fraternity.

This is why the French have so many festivals (fêtes). All over the country and all year round, entire towns and villages will be having a party, which can last for days and always ends up looking one way or another like the great feast with which every Asterix adventure ends: fires, roasts, music and drinking.

Ostensibly, these fêtes are supposed to celebrate something specific – the storming of the Bastille, the birth of someone local who became famous, or the time when Gaston found the €2 coin he'd lost down the back seat of his 2CV. In fact, of course, all fêtes are held to celebrate the same thing: being French.

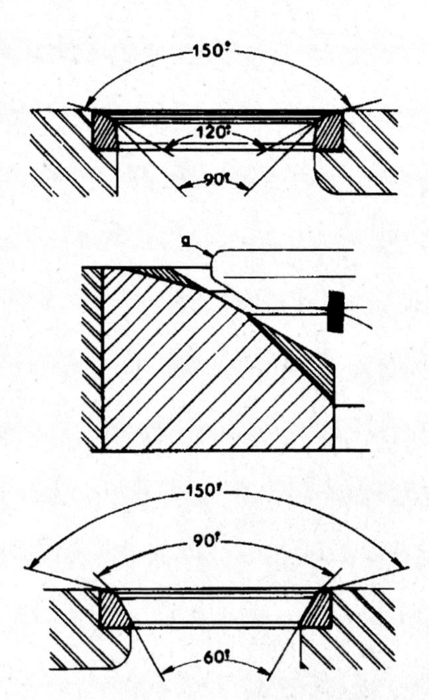

FIG 7•8 **BRIDGING THE GAP BETWEEN PERCEPTION AND REALITY**

Other nations don't see the French the same way the French see themselves. This doesn't bother the French one bit, because they know they're right and everyone else is wrong.

 Finance deals

The French do business in very different ways to the British.

a) They are inherently mistrustful of accountability. The French believe that anyone they answer to will only ever criticise and never praise. Better by far not to answer to anyone at all, and to do one's job well enough to stay under the radar but not so well that people notice.

b) A meeting will start 15 minutes after it's supposed to, in order to allow those who are late to get there. This is entirely standard and known as le quart d'heure marseillais/parisien/wherever. This author has turned up on time for a business lunch and sat there like a lemon for exactly 15 minutes before the French arrived, full of bonhomie and handshakes.

c) They're inherently negative. They'll pick holes in a proposal long before they assess its upside. Part of thls Is thelr natural pessimism; another part is that they don't want to look stupid or naïve by rushing into something, and that if they point out defects then they look intelligent and worldly.

d) They don't believe in win-win. Probably something to do with winning being an alien concept in the history of French warfare. They're very zero-sum about the whole thing: if one party wins then the other party by definition must lose. Only when the Frenchman has won does he feel happy. The trick is therefore to make him feel as though he's won, even though he might not actually have done so.

e) They hate the fact that English is the international lingua franca. They're very proud of their language and honestly believe it to be the best in the world. If you try and speak to them in even basic French, they won't laugh at you; they'll appreciate the gesture.

f) Most French companies are run along very formal and hierarchical lines. A Frenchman who says he has to run a proposal up the chain of command is not fobbing you off: he really has to do that, no matter how much he might dislike it.

g) The quickest way to get a Frenchman to do something is to suggest, in the nicest possible way, that he's incapable of doing it.

Exterior

How the French see the British

It's broadly true but overly simplistic to say that the French take a dim view of the British. They take a dim view of the English. The Scots they rather like.

In no particular order, here are ten French boeufs with les rosbifs:

1) Warm beer.
2) L'albion perfide, for our having allegedly poisoned Napoleon.
3) And having sentenced Joan of Arc to death.
4) The fact that English and not French is the world's lingua franca. Even though this is much more down to America than the British. The British conquered America once upon a time, so it's all the Brits' fault anyway.
5) Brexit.
6) Badly dressed.
7) Poor, stodgy food.
8) Sexually repressed.
9) Every single expat who ever read Peter Mayle and paid too much for a ruin in an idyllic part of France.
10) Poor transport systems (Eurostar trains go noticeably quicker on the French side of the Channel than on the English).

There are more than 250,000 French people living in London. The last time so many French people came to Britain was in 1066, and they landed a little further south.

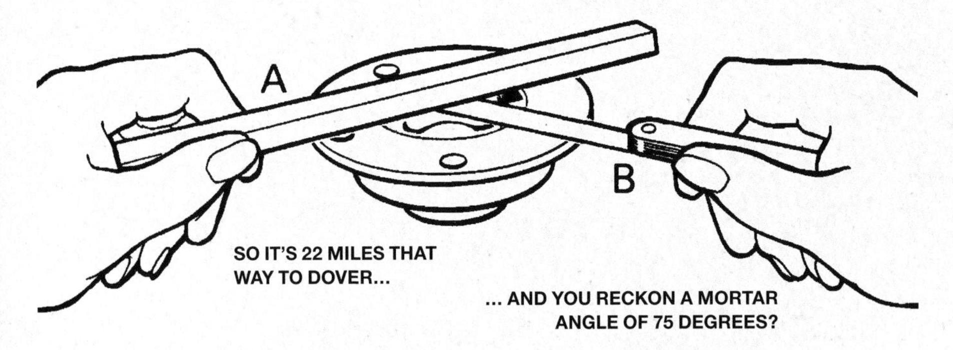

FIG 7•9 **PREPARING THE WEAPONRY AT CALAIS**

How the French see the Germans

The French view the Germans with a mix of 90% resentment and 10% resentment. They envy the Germans' economic success and hate the guttural harshness of their language – if French is the language of love, then German is that of forced marches and throat-clearing.

It's bad enough to have your next-door neighbour be the dominant force in Europe but even worse when that self-same neighbour is manifestly less cultured, less handsome, less cool and has substantially less panache than you do. For the French, Germany is the geopolitical version of the nerd who ends up with the girl, and they can't stand it.

'In Germany, they consider beer to be a vegetable,' said French writer Jean-Marie Gourio. His fellow author Jean Mistler weighed in with the view that 'Europe would be almost complete if the French stayed one less hour in the bistro and the Germans stayed one more hour in bed.'

How the French see the Americans

The French admire the Americans for many things: their success, their innovation, their optimism. Young French people listen to American music on American smartphones and wear American clothes to watch American films – a mass cultural invasion which alarms many older French people.

This entire struggle is centred on Marne-la-Vallee, better known as Disneyland Paris. Here, American culture in all its Mickey/Minnie/princess can-do glory runs smack bang into French ideas of customer service (optional) and cynicism (high). For the first few months of its existence Disneyland Paris didn't even have an alcohol licence, until it became clear that no self-respecting Frenchman could be expected to trog round an amusement park all day without a fortifying carafe of vin rouge or three.

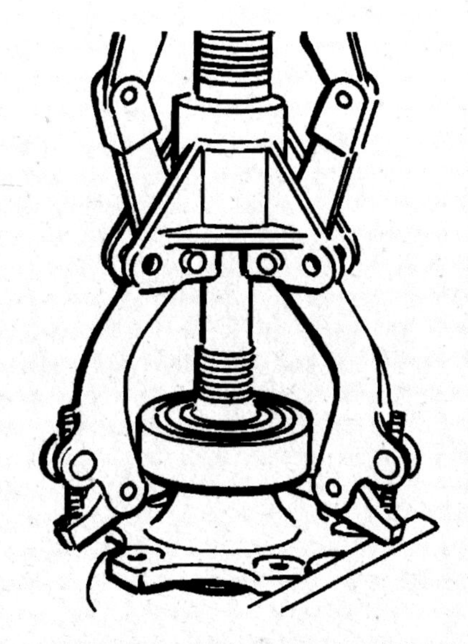

FIG 7•10 **FRANCE'S GREATEST CONTRIBUTION TO THE WORLD: THE CORKSCREW**

Model history

The history of France is a long and distinguished one. The single most famous event is probably the French Revolution, which spawned the phrase 'liberté, égalité and fraternité' – a slogan the French were pretty pleased with until they realised they could, and perhaps should, have gone for 'sex, drugs and rock n' roll', 'rum, sodomy and the lash' or 'wine, women and song'.

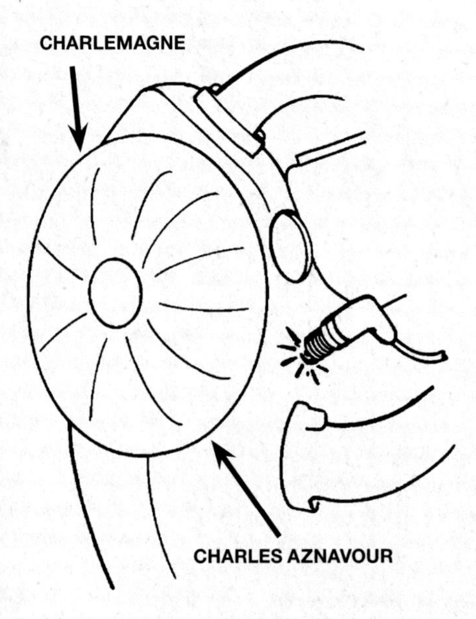

FIG 7•11 **THE ENDLESSLY TURNING WHEEL OF FRENCH HISTORY**

c. 500 BC

Greek sailors arrive and settle in what will eventually become Provence. Foolishly, their chief scribe Petros Maylos chooses not to write a whimsical account of his year in Provence poking good-natured fun at the locals, thus missing out on selling millions of copies and having his book turned into a BBC mini-series starring John Thaw and Lindsay Duncan.

58-51 BC

Roman forces under Julius Caesar conquer Gaul. All of Gaul? No: one village still holds out. It is two millennia before the stories of Asterix and Obelix are unearthed for a modern audience.

800 AD

Charlemagne is crowned
(a) Holy Roman Emperor and
(b) Best Child-Namer for the nomenclature of his sons Pippin the Hunchback and Louis the Pious. Louis keeps the tradition going with two of his own sons, Charles the Bald and Louis the German, thus establishing a tradition which lasts through Louis the Fat, Louis the Quarreller, John the Posthumous, Philip the Tall, Charles the Mad, Charles the Well-Served, Louis the Prudent and Charles the Affable.

1643 – 1715

Louis XIV reigns. Rebrands himself the 'Sun King' after an image consultant advises him to 'keep it light, keep it bright.' Creates a centralised state and weakens the aristocracy, thus consolidating a system of absolute monarchical rule supposedly granted by divine right. A Frenchman who thinks he's God: who'd have imagined it?

1775

Marie Antoinette, told that the peasants have no bread, says 'let them eat cake.' This statement was brought to you in association with Mr. Kipling and his exceedingly good cakes, though it is still some years before product placement truly catches on.

1793

One of the French Revolution's leaders, Jean-Paul, Marat, is assassinated in the bath. There is no truth to the rumour that his demise persuaded his fellow countrymen that the bath is a dangerous place and one to be avoided at all costs.

1800s

Napoleon introduces the Napoleonic code of law recognising the principles of civil liberty, equality before the law, and the secular character of the state. He also institutes an efficient tax system and enforces meritocracy in the armed forces.

1814-30

The Bourbon restoration. Sadly for all concerned, nothing to do with either whisky or chocolate biscuits which are excellent when dunked in tea (the biscuits, that is, not the whisky, though come to think of it whisky dunked in tea has its merits too.)

1889

Gustave Eiffel builds a tower as part of the Exposition Universelle. Given that this is an enormous erection which was never meant to last but is still standing proud today, he may also have unwittingly stumbled across Viagra. The tower is more than 300 metres tall and Eiffel lives in an apartment right at the top. He finds this in general a pleasing experience – nice to get away from it all, and of course no-one has better views than he has – but on the days he opens his front door and only then realises that he's forgotten the milk, it's a right pain in the derriere.

1944

Special Operations Executive Nancy Wake parachutes into the Auvergne region to help the Resistance. Her parachute gets stuck in a tree as she lands, and the Frenchman who helps her down says 'would that all trees could bear such beautiful fruit.' Nancy is unimpressed. 'Don't give me that French shit,' she replies.

Previous models

Joan of Arc (1412-1431)

Joan is a peasant girl who claims to have received heavenly visions telling her to reclaim France from English control during the Hundred Years' War. In an early example of French gender politics, she has to work hard to get the men to believe her, and even when she's done so she's forced to disguise herself as a man to make it to the front line. She's instrumental in persuading King Charles to claim the crown at Reims, a show of support for which he shows his appreciation by abandoning her to the English the following year. In their desperation to convict her, church officials charge Joan with 70 counts, including witchcraft, heresy, dressing like a man and not knowing the words to Charles Aznavour's Greatest Hits.

Charles de Gaulle (1890-1970)

The dominant force of wartime and postwar French politics. Maintained the spirit of splendid French contrariness by withdrawing France from NATO and blocking Britain's entry into the Common Market (thus making him history's first Brexiteer). Survived several assassination attempts from right-wing paramilitaries and Edward Fox. Drove a Citroen DS, very probably the coolest car in history. Not for nothing when he died did President Pompidou say simply 'General de Gaulle is dead. France is a widow.'

Charles de Gaulle is now an airport outside Paris whose most famous resident was the Iranian refugee Mehran Karimi Nasseri, who spent 18 years there and whose story inspired the Tom Hanks film 'The Terminal.'

CHECK-IN STAFF: ABSENT DUE TO RISE OF THE ROBOTS

GROUND CREW. ***ABSENT DUE TO REFUSING TO WEAR UNSTYLISH HI-VIS VESTS***

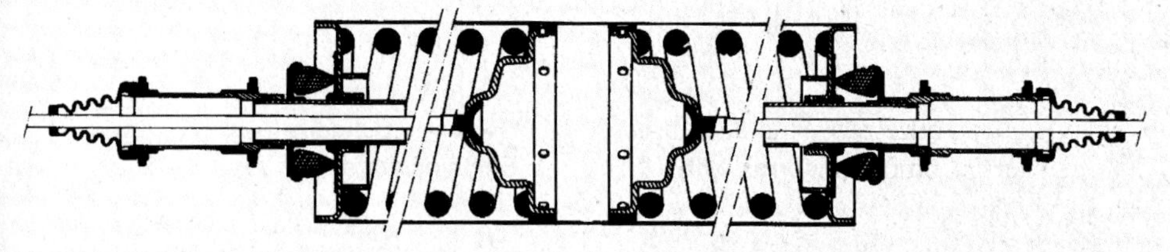

BAGGAGE HANDLERS. ***ABSENT DUE TO LUNCH***

PASSPORT CONTROL. ***ABSENT DUE TO SCHENGEN AGREEMENT***

FIG 7•12 **EMPLOYMENT DEMOGRAPHIC SCHEMATIC, CHARLES DE GAULLE AIRPORT**

Jean-Paul Sartre (1905-1980)

Philosopher, playwright, novelist, wearer of black polonecks, smoker of unfiltered Gauloises, and up there as a contender for The Most French Person Who Ever Lived. He coins the phrase 'hell is other people', presumably after a ride on the Paris Metro during rush hour when his fellow passengers' underarm microbes are celebrating the arrival of spring. Captured by the Germans during World War Two, he proves himself impervious to interrogation by turning his captors' questions back on them. 'What is a name? What is a rank? What is a serial number? They are nothing more than society's attempts to classify the unclassifiable and diminish our individuality.' In later life he renounces literature on the grounds that 'it functions ultimately as a bourgeois substitute for real commitment in the world.' Of course it does.

Eric Cantona (1966-)

'1966 was a great year for English football,' proclaims the Nike advert. 'Eric was born.' Cantona is a Cavalier amongst Roundheads. On arrival at Leeds, he's puzzled by the fans turning up in army combat uniforms with camouflage cream on their faces. He's expressed in a TV interview his appreciation for the French poet Arthur Rimbaud: they think he's referring to Vietnam veteran John Rambo.

THIS IS A BOLT

THIS IS B BOLT

FIG 7•13 **THESE ARE TWO BOLTS. NEITHER OF THEM ARE CALLED USAIN.**

The collar of his football shirt permanently turned up, back ramrod straight and chest puffed out, even Cantona's penchant for chunky Starsky-style cardigans off the pitch can't dent his cool. He launches himself into the crowd at Selhurst Park to kung-fu kick a spectator who's been abusing him and, on being banned for eight months, holds a press conference so magnificently French it could have been scripted by Sartre himself.

Eric enters. Eric sits. The journalists shout questions. Eric holds his hand up. The journalists fall quiet. Eric speaks.

'When ze seagulls follow ze trawler...'

Eric sips water.

'...it's because zey zink sardines will be thrown into ze sea. Zank you very much.'

Eric stands up. Eric leaves.

Legendary.

Vehicle regulations

The French adore the state. They believe that the State not only can fix everything but also that it should. A huge proportion – almost a third – of French adults work for the state in one way or another, and being a civil servant is seen as esteemed and desirable. Public-sector workers in France work round the clock, from 9am to 1pm.

This national love for the state and all that sail in her leads inevitably on to perhaps the biggest bane of life in France… the bureaucracy. The following tips may help you. A little.

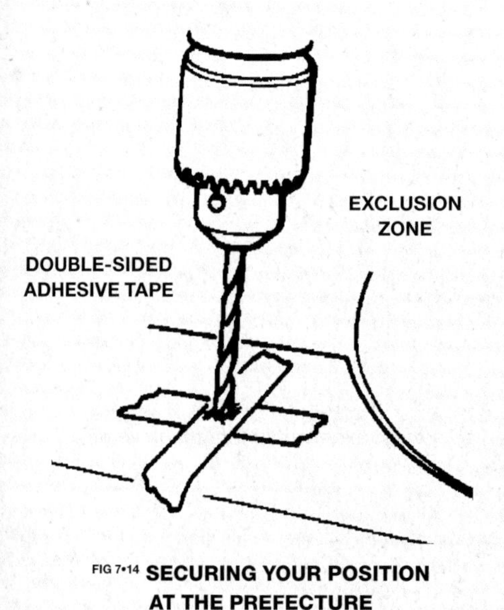

FIG 7•14 **SECURING YOUR POSITION AT THE PREFECTURE**

1) Passport, birth certificate, driving licence, electricity bill, your old student ID, your old fake student ID, your one-day pass for Disneyland Paris… if you own it, copy it. Ten times. No photocopier manufacturer has ever gone bust in France.

2) Have a pen to hand. When you're not signing forms in triplicate, you'll be doodling to while away the hours of waiting. When you're not doodling to while away the hours of waiting, you'll have gone half mad and be writing **ALL WORK AND NO PLAY MAKES JACQUES A DULL BOY** over and over.

3) Don't try and be too clever about dates. If something expires on a certain date, there's only one time to do something about renewing it, and that's on the day itself. Going a month early, a week early, a day early…. non, non, non.

4) While you shouldn't be a day early, nor should you be a minute late. Bureaucracy is run for the bureaucrats' convenience and not your's. On the day itself, get there early. Like real early. Like camping out on the street the night before the Black Friday sales early.

French bureaucracy

A *Turn up at Prefecture three hours ahead of time.*

Take ticket. Find that there are 80 people ahead of you even though it's only 6.30am Wait in line with growing feeling of mania.

Number 81 finally comes up. You are directed to counter number 4.

Reach counter no. 4. Find counter no. 4 closed as Jean-Baptiste who works there has just gone for lunch.

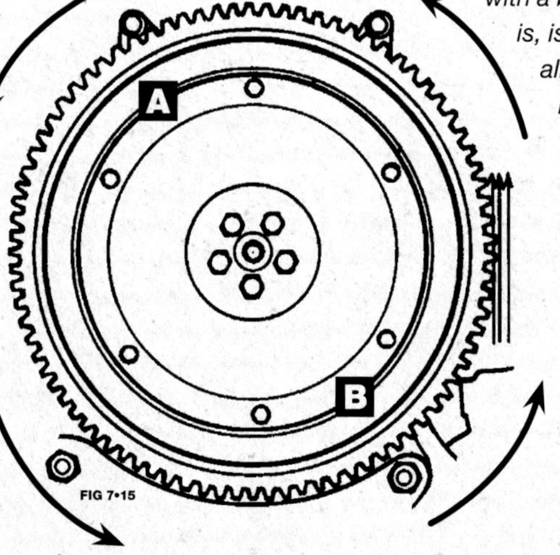

Take another ticket. Find you're now number 623. Weep quietly. Empires rise. Empires fall.

B *Number 623 comes up. Go to counter no. 4. Yes, Jean-Baptiste had a most excellent lunch, thank you for asking. Hand Jean-Baptiste all your papers. Watch with sinking feeling as Jean-Baptiste frowns. 'Zees document 'ere, zis is not the right one. We need your school report from ze winter of Year 4, not ze summer of Year 5.' 'But that was 30 years ago!' Shrug. Bof. Bien sur.*

Go home. Get right school report. Return. Fill in form.

Go to another building three metro stops away. Hand in form.

Return to Prefecture. Explain that you need to have a rental agreement authorised. Discover you can't have a rental agreement without having a French bank account. Discover you can't have a French bank account without providing a local mobile number. Discover you can't have a local mobile without a rental agreement. Weep again. Exclaim 'but that's.... that's....!' 'Yes,' replies Jean-Baptiste with a beatific smile. 'It is, isn't it?" Rip up all forms. Return home. Get very drunk.

Fuel economy

The French attitude towards money (as opposed to Monet, whom they all love, though the true connoisseur arguably prefers Manet), is a world away from the American and the British.

The Americans love being rich and want everyone to know that they are. An American who sees someone driving a Ferrari will be genuinely admiring of him. The British love being rich and want everyone to know that they are, but pretend that they don't. A Brit who sees someone driving a Ferrari will make a hand gesture implying that the driver has more than a nodding acquaintance with self-abuse.

The French are very ambivalent about being rich and don't want anyone to know that they are. A Frenchman is very unlikely to see someone driving a Ferrari unless he's on the Cote d'Azur in summer (and even then it will probably be a Russian driving the Ferrari rather than a Frenchman).

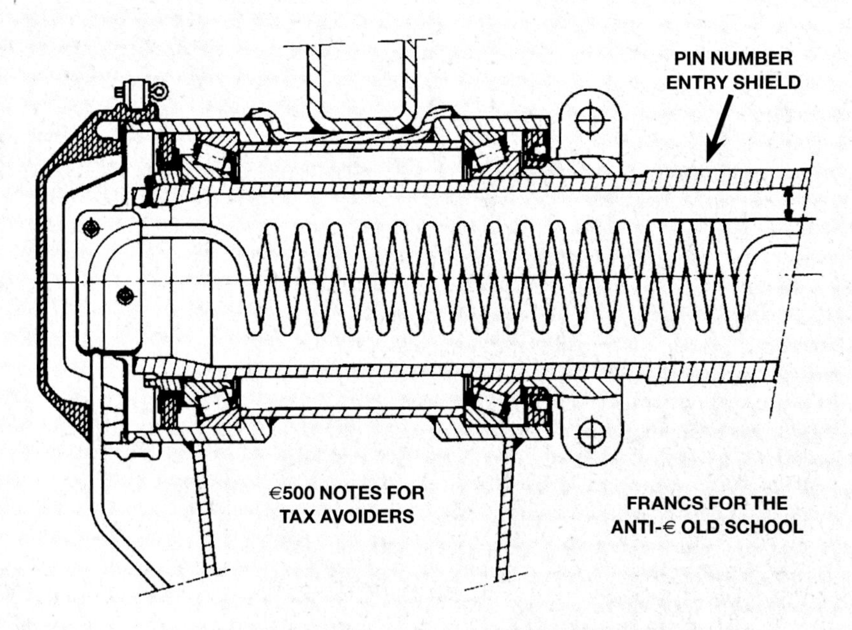

FIG 7•16 **FRENCH AUTOMATIC CASH DISPENSING MACHINE**

⚠ Customer service

The customer is king

The Anglo-Saxon idea that the customer is king is anathema to the French. You should count yourself lucky that the Frenchman lets you into his shop and allows you to buy his products. He's offering expertise in his field, be he the butcher, the baker or the candlestick maker, and he expects you to recognise this. If you ask for something and he suggests something else, it's because his suggestion will suit you better than what you originally asked for. The customer is always right? Make sure the door doesn't smack you in the arse on your way out, won't you?

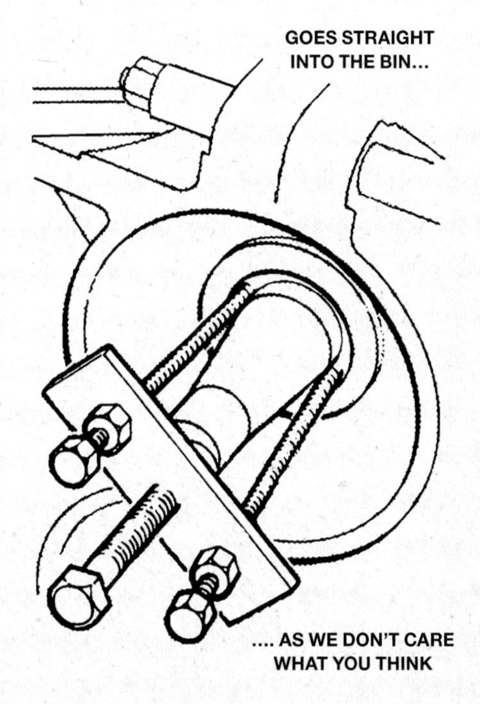

FIG 7•17 TYPICAL CUSTOMER FEEDBACK MECHANISM

Public Holidays

French public holidays are on a Thursday for a very good reason. This renders the Friday pointless as a work day, therefore allowing everyone to take a four-day weekend. They even have a name for this: faire le pont, make the bridge.

Business Hours

Don't try and call a French business contact outside business hours. The French are militant about the work-life balance, and relaxation is considered not just desirable but vital. If you send emails at midnight, they'll think you're drunk, deranged or insomniac, none of which they will approve of. Work is work. Life is life. The French don't confuse the two.

Other countries could learn a lot from the French on all these points.

Language selection

Ah, the French language. The language of love. The language of sensuality. The language of the gods. But unfortunately for the French, not the language of the world. Cultured Russians may have learnt French in Tolstoy's time, but nowadays they're too busy learning English, especially the phrases 'yes, young Nikolai has got into Eton' and 'I haven't heard from Gennady since he was summoned back to Moscow by the Kremlin just last week.'

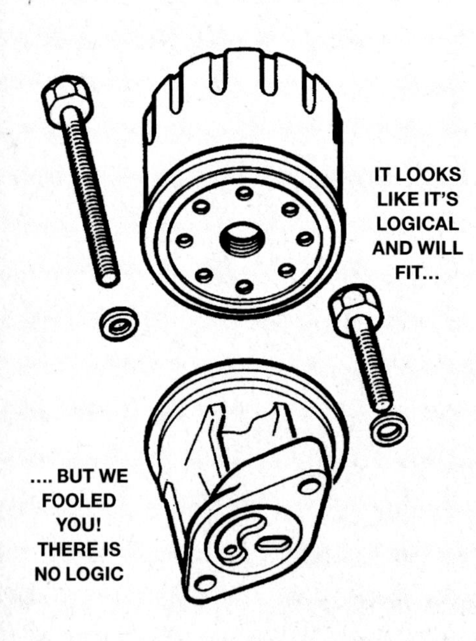

FIG 7•18 **FRENCH LANGUAGE SCHEMATIC**

1) When it comes to giving the scores for the Eurovision Song Contest, every single nation gives theirs in English apart from one. Yes, you guessed it. Like Asterix' village in occupied Gaul, the French hold out.

2) The French don't sign letters with a simple 'best wishes' or, even worse from their point of view, 'cheers'. They give it the full 'veuillez accepter mes sentiments bien profonds', even if you've never met them and/or they're demanding money with menaces.

3) Numbers. It's simple enough in English. Sixty. Seventy. Eighty. Ninety. One hundred. Not so for the French. Sixty. Sixty ten. Four twenties. Four twenties ten. One hundred. What's all that about? If Jay-Z was French, he'd be telling the world that he's got four twenties ten and nine problems and the way his language counts is definitely one.

4) Noun genders. Totally incomprehensible to English speakers. Le Tour de France (bike race) is masculine, but La Tour Eiffel (Eiffel Tower) is feminine. How on earth can a giant phallic symbol be feminine? Why, France? WHY?

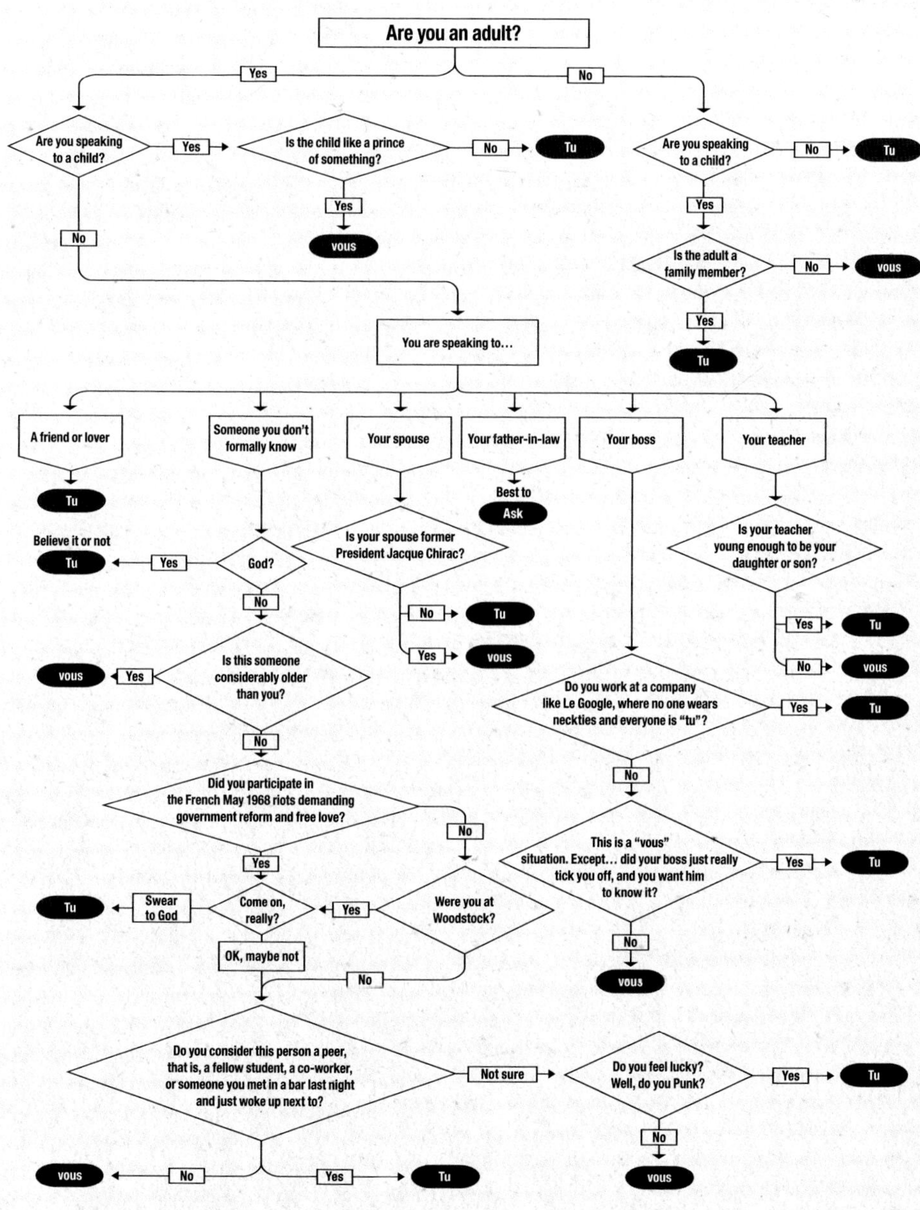

Excerpted from *Flirting with French: Adventures in Pursuit of a Language*, by William Alexander (Duckworth, 2015). WilliamAlexander.com

Fuel

The only piece of furniture as important to a Frenchman as the marital bed (or the extra-marital bed) is the table. Food and drink for the French is a matter of pleasure rather than just function. UNESCO has declared French gastronomy one of the world's cultural treasures, like Angkor Wat or the Tower of London.

If it walks, runs, crawls, swims or flies, the French will eat it, and not just bits of it too – almost all of it, including entrails, brains, tails, ears, hooves and parts even more unmentionable. The French are omnivores in every way.

Boudin noir (pork blood), tête de veau (calf's head), oursins (sea urchins) and of course escargots (snails) all appear on French plates and disappear just as quickly down an appreciative French gullet.

On a French film or TV set, everything stops during lunch, through legal requirement as much as custom.

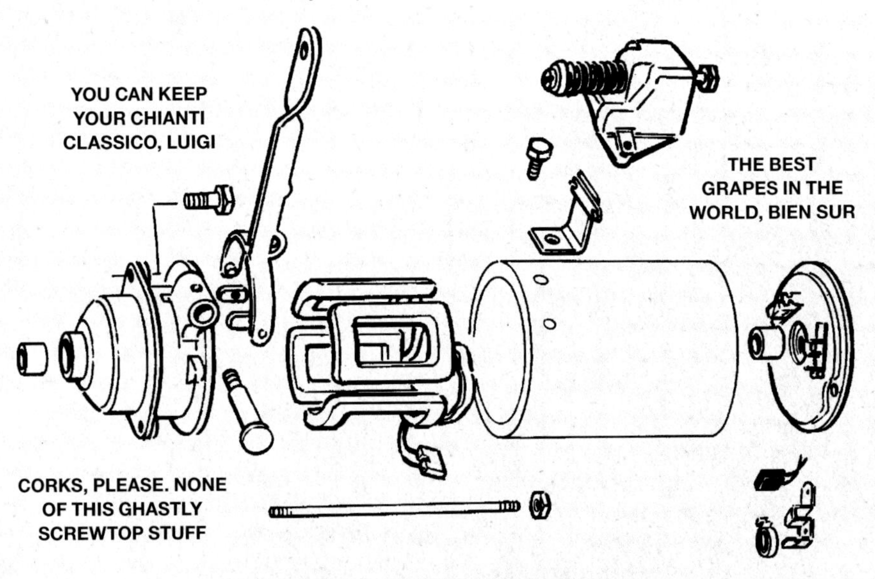

FIG 7•19 **THE FRENCH WINEMAKING PROCESS**

 Staples of the French plate

The baguette

Ten billion – ten billion! – baguettes are made and eaten in France every year. For the French, the baguette is a multipurpose item, a sort of culinary Swiss Army knife. A baguette can accompany anything and everything. It can be slathered with butter and jam and dipped into coffee at breakfast (this being France, of course, coffee is served in bowls). It can have squares of chocolate studded into it to make an impromptu pain au chocolat. Hell, if *Star Wars* had been French, they'd probably have fought with baguettes rather than light sabres.

Cheese

The average Frenchie eats a kilo of cheese every fortnight. They never eat it as an appetiser or on cocktail sticks, which they regard as a habit strictly for barbarians and Americans (as far as the French are concerned, of course, there is considerable overlap between the two groups). Nor do they eat it at the end of a meal as the British do. For the French, cheese has one place and one place alone: after the main course and before dessert. They never say a cheese stinks, even if its odour is so pungent that it could double as a weapon of mass destruction, they admit only that a cheese is 'strong'.

Wine

The French drink more alcohol than any other nation in the world bar one (Luxembourg), though outside of fêtes you rarely see a legless French person, and certainly there's almost no culture of binge-drinking as in, oh, any British town or city on Friday and Saturday nights. Or on Sunday, Monday, Tuesday, Wednesday and Thursday nights, come to think of it. The French drink red wine with food and never on its own. They never buy the cheapest wine possible, as they sincerely believe life's too short to drink bad wine. When pouring wine, never (a) fill a glass to the brim (b) let the wine drip down onto the maker's label. Although the French haven't used the guillotine for many years, they reserve the right to bring it back for crimes against humanity such as these.

WARNING

There's none of this grab-a-sandwich-on-the-run malarkey you find in London or New York. The French don't fit meals in around the rest of their lives: they fit the rest of their lives in around meals.

Sportscars

Tour de France

The quintessential French sporting event is, of course, the Tour de France. As much travelogue as bike race, it lasts three weeks in July, makes insane demands of its participants, and brings millions of spectators to the roadside for several hours of waiting and then fifteen seconds of action. Nowhere outside the French bedroom is the ratio between anticipation and actuality so marked.

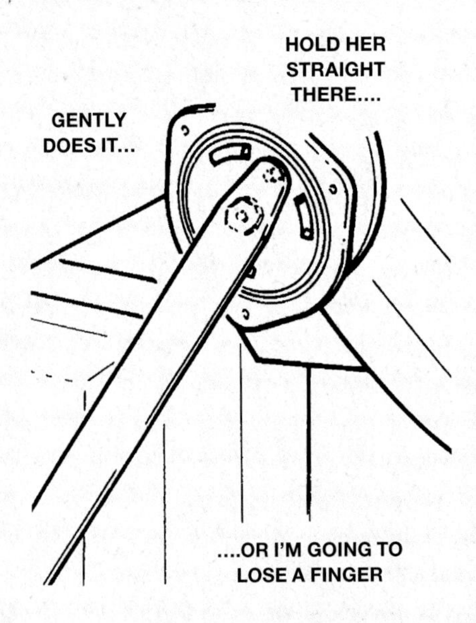

FIG 7•20 **FIXING A TOUR COMPETITOR'S BRACKET ON THE FLY**

Rugby

French rugby is schizophrenic. The forwards tend to be savage hulks from the south-west with faces like Easter Island statues and a Terminator-style imperviousness to pain: they've been known to break their own noses before a game by headbutting the dressing-room wall to get them in the mood. The backs, on the other hand, look as though they've just stepped off a catwalk, sometimes literally: former centre Franck Mesnel now runs a boutique. Mesnel played for Racing Club de Paris, who were notorious for drinking champagne at half-time and dressing up as pelote players or in pink bow ties. You can perhaps envisage Martin Johnson running a boutique or wearing a pink bow tie, but not in this world or any conceivable parallel one.

The acme of French rugby flair came in the semi-final of the 1999 World Cup. They were 14 points down to the All Blacks when they suddenly decided to start playing properly. In a whirlwind of staggeringly beautiful rugby, they scored 33 points without reply to win a famous victory. Even their captain, Raphael Ibanez, seemed nonplussed afterwards. 'The only explanation', he posited, 'is that we are French.'

Reassuringly, they got thrashed a week later in the final against Australia.

Football

Football. Like England in 1966, France won the World Cup they hosted (1998). Unlike England, they have actually vaguely looked like repeating that triumph (they reached the final in 2006), and they also won Euro 2000. The lynchpin of both these victories was Zinedine Zidane, who is up there with Socrates and Johan Cruyff as the coolest man ever to play football.

In fact, French footballers are in general pretty cool. Apart from Cantona (see Famous Models), there's also Emmanuel Petit ('he's French, he's slick, his name's a porno flick'), Thierry 'what's the French for va-va-voom' Henry and Lilian Thuram, who (a) carries off a girl's name with considerable aplomb (b) played 142 times for France but scored only two goals, both of them in a World Cup semi-final.

Cricket should by rights be a French sport: the rules are impenetrable and the fact that five days' contest can end without either side winning appeals to the French sense of contrariness.

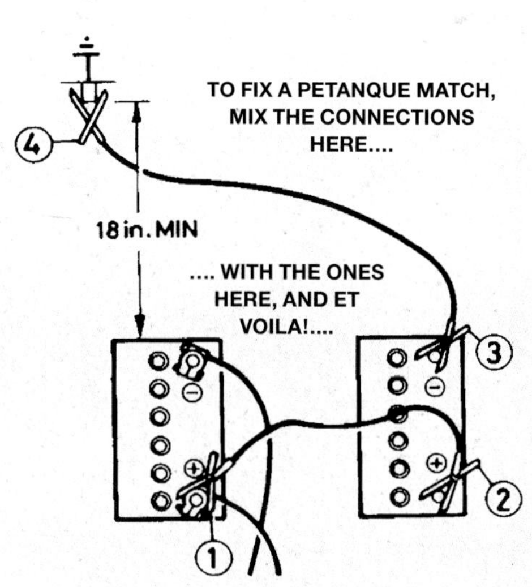

FIG 7•21 **.... THE PETANQUE SCOREBOARD READS 13-0 IN YOUR FAVOUR**

Petanque

The appeal of petanque to the French is clear. It can last several hours, thus affording plenty of opportunity for talking, gesticulating, arguing and drinking. It has its own arcane and amusing terminology, such as 'to fanny' (mettre fanny), when one team fails to score and loses 13-0. Most of all, cheating's positively encouraged. Subtly rolling the boules with your foot, scraping the ground where you wish your boule to land, trashtalking, standing in your opponent's eyeline, distracting your opponent as he's about to play… these are the trademarks of the successful player, and they are lauded rather than criticised.

Vehicle manual

Marcel Proust

What they say: 'Proust's *In Search Of Lost Time* is an epic masterpiece.'

What they mean: 'It's very long and we didn't understand most of it.'

What they say: 'Rather than a linear narrative, life becomes a contemplative act constantly tied up with the past through the evocative power of memory.'

What they mean: 'I'm on page 620 and so far literally the only thing that's happened is that someone has got out of a car.'

Victor Hugo

Best known for *Les Misérables*, still one of the longest books ever written (if you read a chapter a day it will take you exactly a year) but now better known as a musical and that movie where Hugh Jackman and Russell Crowe compete to see who can sing more out of tune.

Georges Perec

Author of *A Void*, an entire novel which never uses the letter 'e.' Or rather: author of *A Void*, an ntir novl which nvr uss th lttr ''. In othr words, a prfct xrcis in Frnch prtntiousnss. Not recommended for aficionados of the 90s rave scene, freewheelers, beekeepers, or anyone who esteems effervescence.

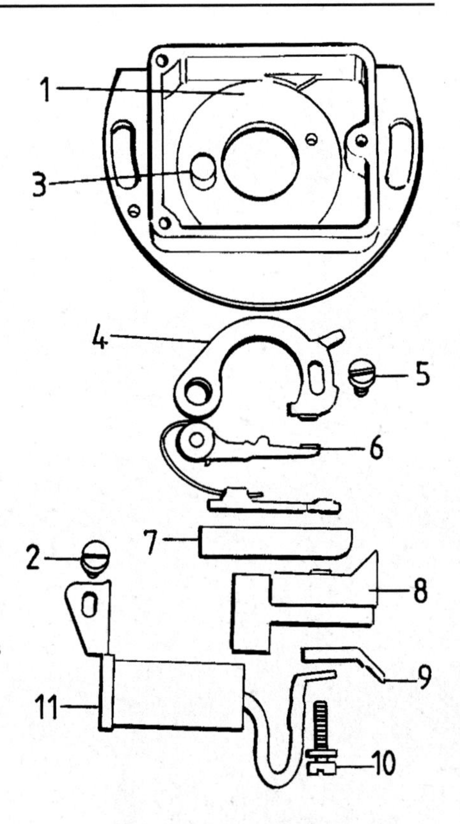

FIG 7•22 **TYPICAL CHAPTER ORDER IN A FRENCH NOVEL. IT'S EXPERIMENTAL, INNIT?**

⚠ French art

French art is as famous as its literature, which is saying something. Perhaps the best-known of all French artists are the Impressionists such as Monet, Manet and Renoir (not to be confused with impressionists such as Mike Yarwood, Rory Bremner and that bloke off *Dead Ringers*).

Before the Impressionists came maybe the most famous French painting of all time: Delacroix's Liberty Leading The People, in which Parisians march forward under the banner of the tricolour representing liberty, equality and fraternity. More cynical observers have noted that Lady Liberty herself is topless and that this alone would have every Frenchman following her wherever she chose to go, as long as they could keep from tripping over their tongues for long enough.

Paris of course also boasts the world's most famous museum, the Louvre. It's a source of mild irritation to the French that the most famous item in there, the Mona Lisa, was painted by an Italian, but they've got their own back by putting it behind bulletproof glass and making sure that there are never fewer than 283 people, all with selfie sticks, jostling each other to see it at any one time.

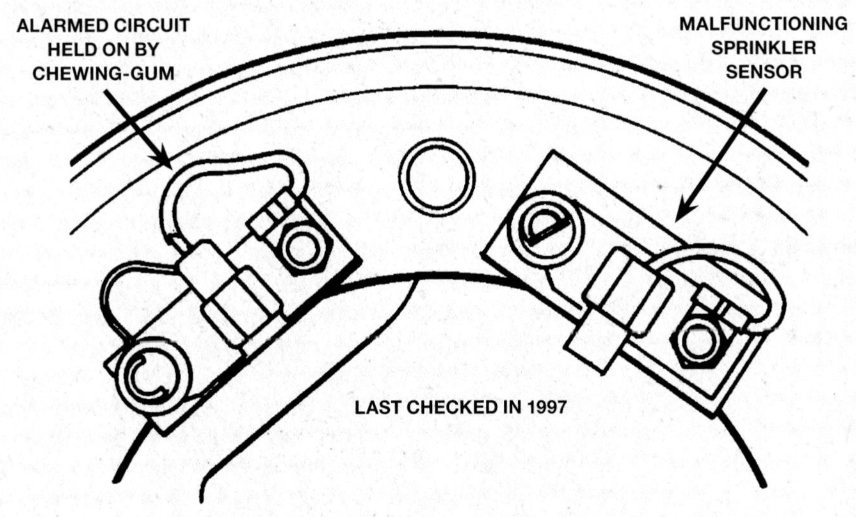

FIG 7•23 **MONA LISA'S STATE-OF-THE-ART SECURITY SYSTEM**

In-car entertainment

Let's get this out of the way quickly: the Marseillaise is the best national anthem in the world. If you can watch the scene in Casablanca when the French sing the Marseillaise over the top of and in defiance of the Germans without either welling up and/or standing to attention, check your pulse. You may be dead.

That apart, French music offers slim pickings. There's Edith Piaf. 'Je ne regrette rien' – not just an all-time classic but a manifesto for being French. There's Daft Punk. And, er, that's about it. Unless you like lounge lizard crooners or rap music which goes 'heep hop heepedy-hop supersexycool oh oh'.

Serge Gainsbourg? The man whose first date with Jane Birkin involved taking her first to a nightclub, then to a transvestite club, and finally to the Hilton where he passed out.

And finally, of course, Johnny Hallyday. The French Elvis, as he must by law be known outside France, though if anything he's more the French Cliff Richard (at least in terms of his music if not his tangled love life). His skin appears to be even more leathery than his trousers, which is no mean feat in itself. He's the Prince of Uncool, but deep down he seems to know this and even to revel in it, which in turn makes it hard to take against him.

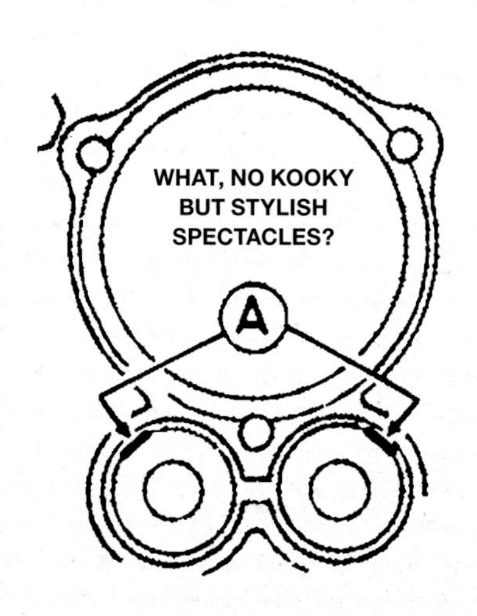

FIG 7•24 **FRENCH CONTACT LENS CASE**

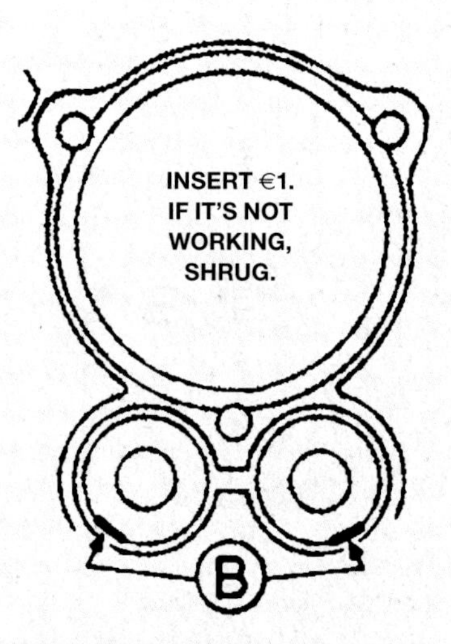

FIG 7•25 **FRENCH PUBLIC BINOCULARS**

⚠ How to star in a French film...

Ah, French films. There's really nothing like them, except of course for other French films. A lot of how-to-write-a-screenplay guides focus on the character's 'journey', the transformative process by which he or she changes from the start of the movie to the end. All characters in French films undergo the same 10-step journey, and they all end up exactly where they began.

a) Light a cigarette. Gaze longingly out of the window.
b) Take clothes off.
c) Quote poetry.
d) Have fight with lover while putting clothes back on.
e) Go for long walk in the rain.
f) Find anonymous letter no-one was ever supposed to read.
g) Be kooky and adorable on the Paris Metro for around 7 minutes.
h) Come across a gypsy/shaman figure who spouts faux-profound gibberish.
i) Deliver monologue about the essential futility of existence.
j) Appear in ending left ambiguous because the director had no idea how to end the movie but hopes that the viewers will see this lack of resolution as intellectual and challenging rather than lazy and half-arsed.

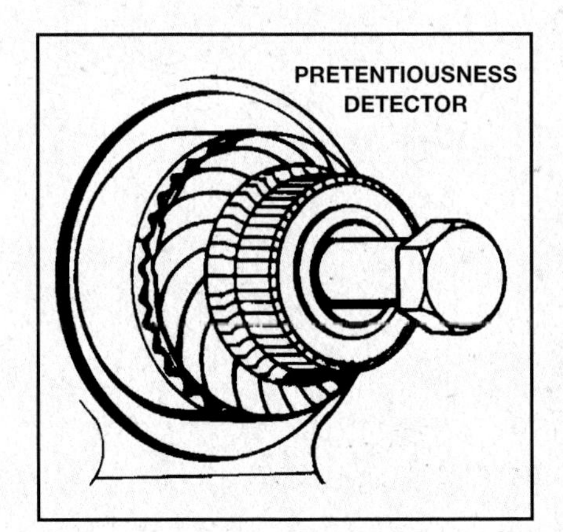

FIG 7•26 **OBSOLETE TECHNOLOGY**

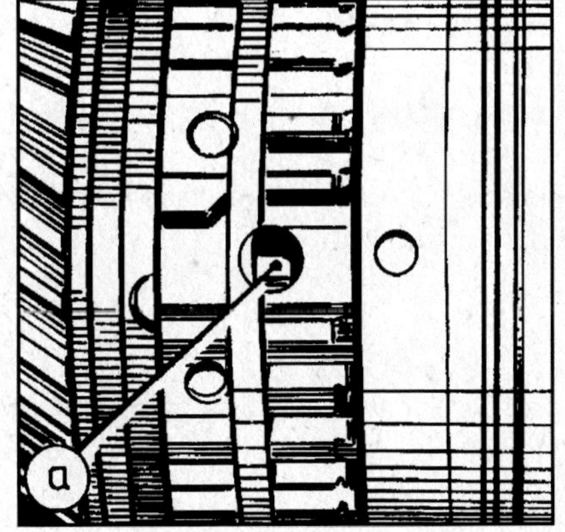

FIG 7•27 **PROJECTOR SET TO SOFT FOCUS**

Fault diagnosis

Fault	Diagnosis	Treatment
Won't speak English	They are French	Condition untreatable
Won't serve Italian wine	They are French	Condition untreatable
Won't serve German beer	They are French	Condition untreatable
Publish long poetry books	They are French	Condition untreatable
Watch pretentious films	They are French	Condition untreatable
Look down their nose at you	They are French	Condition untreatable
Allow poodle to foul the street	They are French	Condition untreatable
Eat well but gain no weight	They are French	Condition untreatable
Try to seduce you	They are French	Condition untreatable
Expect you to seduce them	They are French	Condition untreatable
Look better than you at all times	They are French	Condition untreatable
Lax attitude to marriage vows	They are French	Condition untreatable
Act like speed limit signs aren't there	They are French	Condition untreatable
Refuse to remove black poloneck	They are French	Condition untreatable
Seagulls follow the trawler	They are French	Condition untreatable
No concept of customer service	They are French	Condition untreatable

Conclusion

The French have a reputation for being the most unreasonable nation on earth. In any given situation, the French will almost always behave with maximum regard for their own interests and minimum regard for anything else. Strangely, perhaps, this makes them easy to deal with. A Frenchman will either behave as you expect him to (unreasonably) or better than you expect him to (if he forgets himself for a moment). He will never behave worse than you expect him to. The French can therefore never disappoint you.

And in all honesty a trip to France will never disappoint you either. It's not for nothing that France gets more tourists each year than any other country (and as many as Italy and the UK combined). As a place to visit it's pretty much unparalleled – stunning scenery, beautiful cities, delicious food, exquisite wine and good weather. If you're a culture vulture, an activity freak or a beach bum, there's something for you.

And how can you not love a country which not only has its own rules about kissing (kissing French people, that is, as opposed to French kissing) but also varies them according to where in the country you are? Two kisses (one on each cheek) is usually the minimum number (except for the department of Charente-Maritime where you can get away with one) and standard in the west, east and far south. Three is the norm in the mid-west and southern central areas, four in northern France, and five in Corsica.

Whisper it quietly, but we're a little bit jealous of the French – of their *panache*, their *joie de vivre*, their *savoir-faire* and their *je ne sais quoi*.

Titles in the Haynes Explains series

001	*Babies*	*ISBN 978 1 78521 102 7*
002	*Teenagers*	*ISBN 978 1 78521 103 4*
003	*Marriage*	*ISBN 978 1 78521 104 1*
004	*Pensioners*	*ISBN 978 1 78521 105 8*
005	*Christmas*	*ISBN 978 1 78521 152 2*
006	*Pets*	*ISBN 978 1 78521 153 9*
007	*The French*	*ISBN 978 1 78521 154 6*
008	*Germans*	*ISBN 978 1 78521 155 3*
009	*The British*	*ISBN 978 1 78521 150 8*
010	*Americans*	*ISBN 978 1 78521 151 5*
011	*The Home*	*ISBN 978 1 78521 157 7*
012	*Football*	*ISBN 978 1 78521 156 0*
